BOY THING

Other publications by
John Wedgwood Clarke

COLLECTIONS

Ghost Pot (Valley Press, 2013)
Landfill (Valley Press, 2017)

PAMPHLETS

Sea Swim (Valley Press, 2011)
In Between (Valley Press, 2014)

Boy Thing
John Wedgwood Clarke

2023

Published by Arc Publications,
Nanholme Mill, Shaw Wood Road
Todmorden OL14 6DA, UK
www.arcpublications.co.uk

978 1911469 33 9

Design by Tony Ward
Printed in the UK by TJ books,
Padstow, Cornwall

The cover picture is
'Boy Sheltering his Eyes' by Naomi Frears,
by kind permission of the artist

Arc Chapbook Series
Series Editor: Tony Ward

CONTENTS

I made of silence a porcelain bell,
trapped a fly and waited for it to die.

In the gap between bell and sill,
its feet still move, now, then now.

I
Boy Thing

Our shop is known for the home-cooked hams
my father bags with honey and spice,
floats in the blackened sarcophagus
of the haybox to simmer overnight,
the flame lowered to a blue flutter
as he fits the stainless-steel lid,
seals its edges with canvas wads.

After chapel, he breaks open the tomb,
slumps a ham on the marble counter,
nicks the cellophane bag with the tip
of a knife, the ham juice spurting
like water struck from stone, a gush
he catches in a handleless mug he hands
to me, the fat a golden scurry as I drink.

II

He lets me count the takings. I build him
colonnades of silver and copper,
turn the Queen's head right way up
on crisp and furry banknotes,
sellotape the torn, the biro-tattooed
smelling of sweat and tobacco,
silver thread running through them all.

Numismatist of desire, I slip into
strangers' hands in strangers' pockets
at the dinner table, a market
abuzz with hidden exchange.
He tallies wads against the hollow
clunk of the pricing stamp on tin lids.
What we take pours away like the stream

running under the shop's backroom
where I preside, ensconced
on a throne of cardboard boxes
under flypapers jewelled with flies,
as he raises the manhole cover
and through the iron frame I
see the Stennack race over granite, gold

in the beam of his Ever Ready torch.
It pours on, while he pours away
in the sound of the van before we're up,
off to 'empty the waters' at the shop,
those trays under the fridges
brimful with night's condensation,
edged out and sluiced down the drain.

III

He stoops to it, as if to an oven,
in the tiny office off the stockroom.
Blue-black as the igneous rock
St Ia's Chapel is built upon,
a brass baton-gripping fist sticks out,
knuckles shiny and scarred,

10

as if to let me touch power,
know the weight of paper it contains,
Fire Safe and *Patented* stamped
on a gilded escutcheon plate
like a badge a sheriff might wear.
After everything, it will exist
among ashes and strange voices,
waiting for a shop to rise again.
It shuts with the terrible perfection
of a stone in a pyramid, opens
like the Ark of the Covenant,
or trapdoor in my bedroom floor
through which my father climbs
as I lie feverish, wild flames
singing around his body, my heart
swinging shut as it falls through space.

IV

Black sails turn in the glass flow-gauge.
The generator throbs insurance
against power cuts, sour blows.

Time moves in the shouldered procession
of bacon sides, in torn sheets of buns,
wire's rupture through cheese.

Within the engine's beat, I watch him
bone joints in his study of knives,
clarify rib with cleaver, shin with saw.

11

Heel-pocked linoleum darkens
as his mop flails and the sails turn
like the song of the Little Dutch Boy

I love him to sing – *tick-tock, tick-tock,*
went the funny old clock, and the wheels of the mill
went round and round, and round

went the wheels of the mill – his voice,
in the song's foreverness, a turning pain
as the sails spin forward in the flow-gauge.

V

Between compulsive trips to urinate,
wash my chapped hands raw,
I hold the radio to my ear, turn
the applause of The Proms into static.

The house is quiet but for pebbles
hauled and hushed in the cove
and the meter's wandering tick,
its whirring planetary steel disk.

Deep in police frequencies, I tune
a voice out of the infinite: *he's dead,*
front room, armchair. Airwaves
stare through the man's eyes,

death whispering through the hiss
I erase him to, *now wash your hands of this.*

VI

We run with the dog and stop at the gate
to count the interval between
lighthouse flashes: *one second equals*
one thousand said in your head,

his father told him, his father who worked
on the railways, who said *smoke*
is unburnt diesel, who built him
a model railway in his attic

little trains zip and spark around
through the same tunnel, past the same
trees made of moss and twigs,
life-likeness perfected in the light

at the front of the train, in the dining car
with table lamps and cutlery,
each empty setting identical, a glimpse
of eternity going round and round,

utterly un-enterable as the light
flashes and we stand at the gate, counting.

VII

She bakes a hazelnut meringue,
a strawberry for each of his years.
I like how it cracks and sinks;
she doesn't. I like the raw mix,

the whipped cream. This is
my favourite. She bakes it for him,
a volatile meringue, a wild
meringue, a befitting meringue.

She buys me a book and he
throws the book at us. Forty-seven
sharp hard local strawberries.
Choke on them, why don't you.
The meringue deflates; the whole thing
falls apart, sickly and delicious.

VIII

Mr Linden strikes the tuning fork:
a bee, a bean of sun. He strikes again,
joins it to the table – table glows.

He tests me with slight turns of a peg.
Listen to your tone. Listening is all.
I gaze through the fiddle's f-holes

to the pencil-dry interior, still
as a Middle-European attic room,
the maker's signature missing.

He plays without a shoulder pad,
vibrato into collarbone. I serve him
'tea' – hot water, touch of milk –

for his 'little pill'. When he plays he sways
from the roots of his feet like waves
bowing across the bay, not breaking.

I leave a five-pound note beside his case.
Do you know how many hours that is?
How many deliveries, customers?

I tune his way, listening how
the open strings will find each other,
their perfect intervals a place in which to live.

IX

The bedroom blind bright red, my father
enters the room: *look after her –*
then gently closes the door
on his voice. After he's gone,
my mother won't go out.
Silence swells around us,
twisting each tuft of the carpet
with its long glass songs.

In moments opening between breaths,
within sea-light and shadow,
a soft plague of caterpillars
presses into door jambs,
under window ledges, rims
of empty white-paint tins,
the sky embroidering our house
with secret messages. I learn

plump green-and-yellow bodies,
bristles like first beard-hair,
jaws that make skeletons
of wild cabbage on the headland.

As I touch and stroke their life
into mine, they bunch and knot,
or lift and wave tails as if
magnetised by an invisible source.

Through cracks in days, I gaze
as they horn into armour,
genii slippers, encased storms,
hooked feet blowing into wings.
But some cannot change. Fog swells
and whispers in them, until,
come morning, yellow cocoons dangle
from bodies burst like rotten sails.

    x

We've things out of all proportion, misread
the recipe (to a pint add – not to *every* pint!)
and made our wine a gallon of syrup.
The yeast slows. It slows summer.
The airlock heaves its bubble round the bend
like the thousand-mile digit
in an odometer – look away and you miss it
for another thousand miles.
The lunar-scape inside the demijohn
releases bubbles through the must,
like the paths of ants that feel their way
to clear sweet pools of ant-killer
on the windowsill, abdomens amber
as they sup and take some back for the nest.

XI

The seed so egg-like, something good must come
from weeks suspended over water.

We bought the avocado from Lilliput Stores
where they raffled the chance to blow-up

the power station's stack. Something strikes
the window like a clod of mud. I find the dead

yellowhammer, but can't put it together
with the sound. The taproot aches through air

into water, green breath brewing in its hairs.
I turn the white shoot daily as it sways,

a plate-spinner's stick balancing the sun,
and never see the chimney fall, punched in the gut,

a little smoke whispering from its mouth
as it flops, a blue column of absence in its place.

XII

I plait the Action Men a shelter by the wall
above the cove, tuft grass for fire,
arrange kit bags, canteens, guns,
and leave them, an outpost to think through
into the dark, for night to fill
their hollow bodies with rain.

After inspection, seeds replenished,
I switch their heads until who is who
is no one clear. Summer stares
through drizzle. I withdraw
slug-filled bodies, silvered kit
and jam them in a plastic Chieftain tank.

My brother's made a fire of his bedroom
heaven of Airfix fighters, Humbrol-
painted, decals perfect. The tank
gun wilts, armour loops and sags.
The men born melting from its womb
blur and puddle in the ripping light.

XIII

The spring cuts across the unmade road.
Mica and quartz glint in the lens
it plies in a pothole. After rain,
tadpoles swirl like the tea-leaves
grandma might have read us
if she'd still had a voice. Her body
drowns her slowly through the summer.
She draws us 'flowers', a scattering
of felt-tip jerks across sugar-paper.
The spring flows on into the railway cutting.
On a white plate in an outhouse
the tadpoles are forgotten. Light prints
through wired glass. The air tightens
their final pattern to the pupil of an eye.

XIV

While they divide the house, low-water stillness,
tidal kelp rustle. Where men,
with rods bent double, wrenched water,
lines ripping the surface as they swung
tips above the hidden snag,
fighting for a way out until their lines snapped
and recoiled through rings, I crouch.

Koster, Droppen, Krill – lost lures are gods to me.
I follow curled threads into weed snarls,
crevices, a gleam in a pool
overhung by sea anemones'
spit-silky nipples drip-ringing reflections
they flower under, my ear
water-cupped, arm a tentacle reaching in.

XV

By the kitchen drain I trickle into an empty
dregs from rinsed milk bottles.

She comes out with ashes for roses
swirling about her. Bottles encircle circles

in their wire cage for six
viewed end on, sud-beards dwindling.

I lift and replace them like dolls
with no identity in a family of light.

*

Wheat hisses behind the cul-de-sac.
Rubbish piles at the gate.
She comes out with his marmalade jar
I've seen her stab with scissors.
Wasps spit from bin slits,
tilt for the right to land on its lid.

Like armoured creeping treacle,
meticulous at the edge, they drop
to glass bafflement, rebound
off each other and hard light
down to the heaving yellow rind
where the drowning tread the drowned.

XVI

My crime's a penny I place on the rail
of the coastal branch-line.

In the blare of the two-tone horn
the bay and sky sheer open.

A dark and dripping cliff shudders past.
Blue aftermath, blue aftermath.

Cloud silence. Willow-herb turbulence.
Scattered shit lumps and tissue crust.

Creosote and honeyed tar.
The verb has left the sentence.

Found in the ballast, the penny's
a copper tongue, sunburst portcullis.

XVII

In Sunday School, with the 'Uncle'
who tests milk at the dairy,
we look into Creation
through the big brass microscope
he's brought in for Pentecost
in a black wooden case.

It's tarnished like a trumpet,
old as the foxed engravings
of Wesley in the Men's Room.
He says, no artist, even Leonardo,
made anything as beautiful
as a bird's nest. I stand on a chair

to gaze through its peephole at water
collected from the pond
where we sail our boats on Good Friday,
my eye a blank disk of light
guillotined by a slide,
its spasming stained-glass insurgence,

all bite, fuck and filament,
devouring what heavenly light
of Christ is left in my heart's
wild loud beating,
the green-jewelled watch
unhinged, springs and escapements

tumbling through cold light –
I grasp the microscope
and the jar falls from the table,
a dark shout flung across
the upper room's bare boards
while they all sing on in the faraway chapel.

XVIII

Through the winter a man comes
loping along the branch-line with a can.

He climbs the ladder to the signal by the bridge
and tends its dull red lamp.

How long has he been coming, or someone like him,
along the single track to climb the ladder

to a sign that never changes?
When the light goes out and he does not return,

I look out for him, look through him,
obedient to a rule that's been abolished.

XIX

I know why she's won. When she reads,
the reservoir brightens with fish.
I mouth her word 'creel' like a mystery.

My essay is a digest of armour,
calibre of gun, a dead flotilla of words,
its origin in autumnal gales, sunk.

Ships arrive in the bay like a town
come visiting, steel constellations,
anchor chains land-sliding the night.

Morning brings hollowness beyond
the lighthouse, the Atlantic laid waste.
The ships keep bows to the tide race,

moon dials turning the hours.
Men in yellow cluster and disperse;
one runs the length of a freighter.

Inside rust-streaked superstructures,
they calculate. I don't know how to write
the feeling; how I'm apart with them

looking back at a boy windowed
in a carol of longing, how, next morning,
when the wind drops, I know they'll be gone.

xx

A quartz eye
puckering a slate stone
finds me as I
haunt the winter cove.

It may be the geode
of my dreams.
I want to slice it,
enter pressure

crystals memorise.
It dents the sill,
alone against
glass and trees.

23

To control the room,
I take it to school.
The teacher admires
its purity of form,

keeps it on her desk.
Waves roll me
worrying how I'll ever
again hook fingers

in its eye, feel points
beyond bone
pull in my shoulders,
its head in my hands.

XXI

An assortment of ivory off-cuts
on the table at school break:
he gives me a molar-sized cube,
ridged like a human nail
from the band saw.

Up the Stennack, they slice
piano keys out of the bang
and shudder, the rattle
and craze of flies, burnt-bone-
and-hair stench. The cube

is a chapel of pain, white
as the missionary collection box
in the shape of a church
I take from house to house
silent as wire in a locked piano.

XXII

The light between my hands goes out.
I whisper, but it won't revive.
I swap my daily prayers
for fishing book and tackle shop.

From jewellery carousels of lures
and little chests-of-drawers
in St Ives Sports and Leisure,
I fill the grey compartments of my box

with Clement's booms, beads,
weights like Sputniks, medals, bombs
the rocks dent, fingernails
burr with silvery crescents;

with wire wound tight round cork,
foiled spinners, red feathers,
long and short-shanked hooks
shoaled in photo-album sleeves.

The lives of the fishes and weather
compose my paternosters
flung like wild unstrung pendulums,
flags perfectly swallowed.

Beneath the surface, bait and gleam
signal to names become quick
flicks, shadow deflections
listened to through fingertips,

tensions of emptiness on the lip
of utterance. My lines rise out
tangled, naked, smutted
with reddish beards, and now (barely

registering until it swings
towards me) a small shy portrait
of the seabed, the hook so taken
only the silver eyelet shows

in the fine-boned mouth I
wreck, twisting and wrenching
blood from gills, eyes, my smeared
hands together as I slip it back.

XXIII

Pilchard oil, fish blood, old nets – the spell
breaks as the rod lurches and flies into air
like a sapling, my voice plucked with it:
a white scar in the wake of the mackerel boat.

*

I strike my thoughts into anything but words.
Flames scrunch the crazy Letraset of ants.
Salt halts the slug on its silvery tide. I watch
the sea smash the sun and learn to call it beautiful.

26

XXIV

It comes in the post and stinks to high heaven,
the belt from the Mediterranean
heat of his affair, the belt I slip over
my shoulders on its tightest notch
and drop around me, a hoop
of raw, tan stiffness, ragged on one side,
embossed and compressed smooth on the other.

I wrap it in a bag and hide it like my cut of a crime
that will one day find me out,
its uncured leather a lethal source
men on the news in white overalls and masks
hunt down as they sample and test
the sheep on Anthrax Island,
walking towards the lens and into my silence.

XXV

The Devil can enter you through the TV.
The piano teacher looks into me,
her Coronation pencil poised
to accent. I've watched Salem's Lot.

Dirty-eyed, I've been engrossed
monitoring tension in the frog
at the roadside, what skin can bear
before bones needle through.

His mark is in the syllables
of Ronald Wilson Reagan. I hammer
chords like bell-towers toppling.
I pray to the frog, its lively flesh.

It speaks two flies from its eyes,
a third, I swear, from its mouth.
She changes her son from Pedro to Peter,
practises him three hours a night.

She speaks through him, his fingers
fleeing her in scales, four octaves,
both hands, staccato. That boy is
destined. That boy is filled.

She sharpens her Coronation pencil
in the Empire-State-Building sharpener.
Her pencil never shrinks. *When*
he touches your chest the Holy Spirit

springs in you, flings your body down.
You'll know by this you are chosen.
I whisper to the frog: give me your bones,
give me leaping bones of the spring.

XXVI

He let's me watch him grout the tiles,
caulk joints, hold buckets, arrange
the broken in patterns on a dust sheet.

I try on his face, twitch my nose
the way he twitches his like a rabbit
until I cannot stop and am caught

in the act. I hand him his level.
He hands me doweling so smoothly
machined I grasp I am hands.

I keep it with the granite core sample
from a school trip to the tin mine,
cylindrical white quartz, black-flecked,

my teeth touch for what they are not.
My nose twitches to become anyone.

XXVII

She is 16, he 47 – numbers
that won't stop touching, stay subtracted.

My friend's mother asks,
Is he still with his Fancy Woman?

Her words blow the kitchen from her kitchen.
They prance, public, pubic,

out of control, a spreading stain
in the streets between Bible Christian

and Fore Street Methodist, Zion
and Bedford Road. I hate her ginger beer,

dark chocolate, house like an oak wood
in a book I am almost part of.

A character has turned around
and thrown me out of the story.

I want to wipe the words from her face,
open the Bournville again.

The chocolate gratings writhe
like maggots in secrecy's opened flesh.

XXVIII

As the rain falls, I sit in the stairwell
and restore his bat, sanding
its amber blade to pale willow,
rubbing linseed into its body,
oil from the rag catching in the dent
left in its spine by the ball
he hit for four with it back-to-front.
He would stoop over me,
smoke and bristles, shaping me
into that moment, my hands
on the bat handle covered by his
as we cut and drove and pulled,
the world before I was born applauding
the man I am part of. I touch
the impact crater of that shot,
a sign of perfect timing I want to
live again in me, for my body

to unfurl like the flowing
letters of *The Autograph* scorched
into wood below the splice.
My shots come too early, too late, hit
air, not ball – soft dismissals
that see me left unpicked. But I
have hidden talent: from the top
of the steps to our house I threw
a pebble at him as he approached,
a giant in sheepskin, and the bay
and sky and hate said yes and smote him
out of the nowhere that is me
– *you could have blinded me* –
the shot I know has driven him away.

XXIX

Earth hums my heart
beating into the shape
of the communal refuse shed.

Blowflies flash
through light blades
like fused-glass asteroids,

their deep-throated
amplified buzz in webs
strung through me.

In the bin-day bins,
Page 3 Girls call
from tea-bag cockled newspapers,

fag ashy, cradling
grapefruit whitely deflating
to sweet soil.

As if all know the look
and order of their waste,
I memorise stratigraphies

of crispy-pancake rind,
fish-finger carapace,
clumped tissue,

reconstruct moments
of disposal after reading
strange matter:

Voyager flies by Saturn's rings;
Diana's silk dress whispers
the steps of St. Paul's;

GOTCHA! explodes into
The Belgrano
lives drowning in

sticky-inked headlines,
in tits slick with baby oil,
pull-out paper flags.

XXX

Everything is wrong with me.
I can't put my finger on it.

In the bathroom's cold laboratory
I look for my disease

in the The Pears Encyclopaedia,
pages thin as the Bible,

its 'great rakes noted for longevity';
its 'prostate', 'syphilis',

'gonorrhoea'. What name am I?
'Penis' whispers down tiled corridors.

'Masturbate' incubates horrid eggs,
desire a nest in flames.

XXXI

He offers me the bag,
glue smeared
in the dark fur
of his upper lip,

and I am joined
to the day's roar,
its strong fist
blooming breath,

scattering us
under wood-hurry,
leaves opening
my head so out

at the source
of hardening glue,
lips at the breast,
amniotic sac,

voices congeal
in stiff afterbirths
among bluebells
and lovely bald tyres.

XXXII

With the butane refill's tip between my teeth,
I press on to the summit of my mouth
filling with high-altitude
hawk spiral, streams raging open

chasms more holes than torrents,
filling gasps with gas,
glorying in ice as if blown
from the shower curtain,

no shower curtain only peaks, there are
no walls only distant
dripping in a toilet cistern
as if the earth in fast thick pants were weeping.

34

XXXIII

Buoyed over the uncapped fuel tank,
petrol beats airy thinness gold;

tins, brushes, screws, swarm
in the galactic lockup,

until the roof sucks away
and concrete laps up around and I'm

going down the sea under everything,
each breath sinking deeper,

the sea interior petrol tinted,
sand rippling the plain I'm walking over

towards the number 99, vast, half-buried,
reaching out to touch and know

one short one short one short of –

II
Fathers & Sons

I

The path goes so close to the cliff edge
the trees thin to boundlessness.
Water sounds into water.
Then the granite well appears,
its clarity placed by pins of rain.

A shadow grows. My father
rides my shoulders, his breath mine.
O father weather. O risen wind.
The path shakes loose. Trees
spring blue raging space I crawl by

as the path unfolds the only way
to the estuary I'm wading into,
the current lifting him, his breath
a seal as it hangs in the tide, drifting
between channel lights towards the bar.

II

I row him to the rocks where we'd fish
from our usual places and look at each other,
heads tilted, as if listening to our lines,
eyebrows asking the other, *do you feel a bite?*

Each listening to his line, it strikes us
it might be thought we're listening to a bite,
as if we had the bite we looked for
in the other, confusing ourselves with hope.

We shake our heads and look down.
The sea slides up, spills back. Rocks dry.
Bubbles rise from swaying oarweed tongues.

The lure, after its long journey, flashes out
of dark so clear it seems I'm looking in the eyes
of a stranger reflected in a stranger's eyes.

III

And then I realise the rock where I've left him
is the same as the one he slipped from
smashing his gold watch. And time

does not stop in that moment so much as circle
like the second hand that went missing,
the face as naked as his now is.

IV

They have held my earlobe reins as I held
onto you swaying like a camel.
Your hair in the wind, as you turned
to look at me, became wings

carrying your head away over the house.
Who knows what mine will do?
I have no coat equal to your sheepskin's
shop-smelling mystery as you

stood by the cliff, spume thrown up
like soft magma from the cove.
It was the last shelter of you I knew,

huddled into its fleece, the inside pocket
an elephant's ear I whispered to,
lanterns swinging on the quay across the water.

V

Grease spattered, suede gone brittle,
it slumps on the packing boxes.
I've carried it too long. I'll take from it

the last two buttons, amber-grey horn,
smooth as the inside of a limpet shell.
I snip and slip its eyes into my pocket.

Gulls empty the sky, their squally cries
loosening my hold on things.
Late heat ticks in the tiles and guttering.
The rowan's full breasts shine.
In the attic bedroom, where the wind's
devouring voice in the throat
of the chimney cried out in them,
I've folded up volcanoes, planets,
Kings and Queens of England,
wedged the mobile in the bin,
ending interminable turnings in the internal
thermals, its stored torsions so
nearly time found reversible.
Blue and white blobs, the cornerstones
of missing stories, diagrams, splotch-beings,
roll to a globe of paint and hair,
a smear of weather. It's too late
to touch-up picked-off wood chip shoals,
herds of animals, hunters, whatever
they saw in them on the edge of sleep.
I stick down the flap of wallpaper
over I am a person pencilled on plaster.
Their beds have gone. Only patches remain
where their heads would have been,
precious heads that made this house
flesh-tender, heads tipped back
as they looped arms round our necks
to hold us, books slipping from hands
to thump the floor above us like ripe fruit,
the whole of us listening for the way they turned.

VII

The force of their breath comes at me,
a blow all through me, my clay
boomed alive. They thump and shake
the old hymns of childhood.
I want to be enfolded in the voices
of the old men down on stage
before the naked pale-oak cross,
singing not for pleasure but in the grip
of salvation, as if song might
carry them through the blank
terror growing louder at night, frail,
swaying, caught up in the chorus,
in the wings of the choir, caught
like soft coral in a wave, swaying,
crying, we'll all be there, we'll
all be there – death bleached. Yes,
yes, I want to be among them, to raise
my hands in old harmonies
of aunties and uncles, pantos, polos
passed down the pew, feet burning
on the hot pipe, the mechanical bellows
in the organ loft a steady heart.
Yes, back in my father's house,
called for and come, chosen and saved,
only my son asks, looking up from his book,
when will it end, all this stuff
you don't believe in, his voice like God
catching me naked, ashamed, angry
in the pitch-pine warmed-up damp
of the chapel, while the voices of the vain
old men sing doubt into certainty.

I'm loosening into the mid-summer morning
an arrangement of light, tree of life,
head in the canopy, feet in the dew,
blocking out fence, wisteria, house,
with T-shirts whose messages are not for me;

with the rippling doors of old white towels
they have passed through and through
in changing moments – wrapped and wriggling
on beaches, singing in the shower
to their own tunes. Their newly adult toes

burst their socks, but those socks are still washed:
who has time to sort the old from the new?
Their drawers are fabric rapids and won't close.
Their minds are on meetings in parks,
being in the crowd and stepping away

to burn in damp grass beside I don't know who.
I grip the aluminium pole, surrounded
with the shape of our lives and feel the wind lift,
morning's trance pass in the rush of leaves,
speculative tendrils, lavender shadows.

The cool white shapes sway and brush against me,
pegs holding edges and my longing
for the weight of their bodies on my belly,
shoulders, knees, as they turn and stream in a flat
and filling dance, the joy I cannot hold.

Words have made of me a porcelain bell
in the shape of a dancing figure.

I ring it – a slight sound. The fly
knocks twice on the glass and is gone.

AUTHOR'S ACKNOWLEDGEMENTS

Thanks to the following editors and publications in which versions of these poems first appeared: *Poetry Ireland*; *The Rialto*; *Modern Poetries 1: Cornish Modern Poetries* ed. Ella Frears and Aaron Kent (Broken Sleep Books, 2022).

I will always be grateful to Jane Haynes, who listened me back into shape when I was a twenty-something, incoherent with shame. My gratitude also to the Helyars poetry group, who welcomed these poems and attended so carefully to their needs. Many of them were begun during research leave funded by the University of Exeter.

I'd particular like to thank Fiona Benson for her kindness, support and advice; and to Jane Feaver and Judy Brown for reading early versions of the collection. It is a great pleasure to have this book published by Tony and Angela at Arc, two people who have done so much to keep us connected with world poetry, and who were such kind supporters of my work for the Beverley Literature Festival, bringing great writers to the East Riding of Yorkshire.

And finally, thanks to Lara Goodband for her love, and her sharp eye and ear.

John Wedgwood Clarke is a poet, prose non-fiction writer and academic. He was born in Penzance and raised in St Ives, Cornwall. He trained as an actor at the Guildhall School of Music and Drama before going on to study literature and complete a PhD in 'Objectivist' poetry at the University of York. He is an Associate Professor in Creative Writing at the University of Exeter.

His first collection *Ghost Pot* was described by Bernard O'Donoghue as a 'masterpiece that rewards continual rereading'. Clarke's poetry often grows out of collaboration with scientists and other artists, and is displayed in art galleries, museums and in the landscape. He has directed major research projects and commissions, including most recently, *Red River: Listening to a Polluted River*, funded by the Arts and Humanities Research Council.

His credits as television presenter and researcher for BBC Four include, *Through the Lens of Larkin* (2017) and *Cornwall's Red River* (2021).